THE LANGUAGE OF FLOWERS

PENHALIGON'S
SCENTED TREASURY
OF VERSE AND
PROSE

EX LIBRIS

....

THE LANGUAGE OF FLOWERS

SHEILA PICKLES

LONDON MCMXC

For my Mother and Sister
In loving memory of my Father

INTRODUCTION

Love's language may be talked with these;
To work out choicest sentences
No blossoms can be meeter;
And, such being used in Eastern bowers,
Young maids may wonder if the flowers
Or meanings be the sweeter.
ELIZABETH BARRETT BROWNING. 1806-1861

Dear Reader,

What could be more pleasurable than receiving an unexpected bunch of flowers? A bunch of bluebells to brighten a breakfast tray, Lily of the Valley to celebrate May Day or a simple posy of wild honeysuckle picked in the hedgerows. How much greater the pleasure may be if the flowers themselves carry a hidden meaning. From ancient times flowers have been symbolic. The Romans honoured their heroes with laurel wreaths and Greek mythology tells how many of the flowers were created. In *Hamlet* Ophelia recites the meanings of the herbs and flowers she carries in her arms, for William Shakespeare was well conversant with their significance. Poets have always extolled the virtues of flowers and since Elizabethan times have written of their meanings, but it was the Victorians who turned flower-giving into an art. Inspired by a book entitled *Le Langage des Fleurs* by a French woman, Madame de la Tour, the Victorians practised the new floral code with the same dedication with which they built their cities and furnished their houses. The choice of flower was all important, but so too was the manner of presentation. If the flowers were upside down the opposite meaning was intended, thus tulips presented with their stems uppermost meant blatant rejection from a lover. If the ribbon was tied to the left, the meaning referred to the giver, if tied to the right, to the recipient. On the other hand she could always respond by wearing the flower in different ways – on her heart of course meant love, but worn in the hair implied caution.

From Candlemas to Christmastide our great wealth of plants can convey our sentiments without recourse to the written word. Ivy may be sent to convey fidelity and combined with a few jonquils would be the request for a *return* to faithfulness. Carnations would be sent by a heartbroken suitor but woebetide the girl who receives Narcissus – the sender will always be more interested in himself. Ardent suitors must beware when selecting their roses, for whilst the Cabbage Rose implies ambassador of love and Rose la France invites the loved one to meet by moonlight, the Yellow Rose means that love is waning.

Nobody appreciated flowers more than Elizabeth Barrett Browning, imprisoned in her sick room for long periods, and she writes with such gratitude for the posies picked for her by her husband Robert Browning. Picking flowers one has grown oneself is a great source of joy and I feel fortunate to have grown up in the country with a large garden. My father, whose passion for gardening has certainly been handed down to his children, would proudly take dinner guests to the greenhouse to show off his latest blooms. They would invariably go home with a bag of ripe tomatoes or a fine cucumber – as great a gesture of loving friendship as any of the flowers in his hothouse. I have dedicated this book to him, together with my mother and sister who have always enjoyed growing and arranging flowers, filling their homes with colour and scent, making them welcoming and very special to me.

Sheila Pickles
Canonbury, 1989.

CONTENTS

ANEMONE
Forsaken

Sweet Flower! that peeping from thy russet stem
Unfoldest timidly, (for in strange sort
This dark, frieze-coated, hoarse, teeth-chattering Month
Hath borrowed Zephyr's voice, and gazed upon thee
With blue voluptuous eye) alas, poor Flower!
ON OBSERVING A BLOSSOM ON THE FIRST OF FEBRUARY. 1796.
SAMUEL TAYLOR COLERIDGE. 1772-1834

HE Anemone is part of the Buttercup family but unlike its sunny cousin, is a sad little flower. Anemones have always been known as Wind-flowers, for the ancient Greeks believed they would only open their petals when the wind blew, and so named them after Anemos, the god of the wind.

Another name that country people use is Candlemas-caps, for they flower by the 2nd of February when Candlemas is celebrated in honour of the Virgin Mary.

Drops-of-snow, Granny's Nightcap and Chimney-smock are other names given to the Anemone, particularly the White Wood Anemone which grows wild in lonely woodland and whose significance is Forlornness.

Another legend tells us that when Venus was weeping in the forest for Adonis, anemones sprang up where her tears fell – perhaps why Forsaken, after all, is the true meaning.

BLUEBELL

Constancy

A filbert hedge with wild briar overtwined,
And clumps of woodbine taking the soft wind
Upon their summer thrones ; there too should be
The frequent chequer of a youngling tree,
That with a score of light green brethren shoots
From the quaint mossiness of aged roots :
Round which is heard a spring-head of clear waters
Babbling so wildly of its lovely daughters
The spreading blue-bells : it may haply mourn
That such fair clusters should be rudely torn
From their fresh beds, and scattered thoughtlessly
By infant hands, left on the path to die.

JOHN KEATS, 1795–1821

*B*LUEBELLS are one of our hardiest wild flowers, faithfully returning year after year, and surely they mean Constancy because of their tenacity once established in a garden. They cover our woods with blue carpets each May but dislike being picked and once gathered, the nodding bells soon droop.

It is sometimes confused with the Harebell or the Bluebell of Scotland which is quite a different plant and part of the *Campanula* family. The genus name is *Endymion* and was so loved by Keats that he named the hero of his poetic romance after it.

CAMELLIA
Perfected Loveliness

Violetta. If that is true, then leave me.
Friendship is all I can offer you.
I don't know how to love,
I couldn't feel so great an emotion.
I'm being honest with you – sincere . . .
You should look for someone else,
Then you wouldn't find it hard
To forget me. . . .

Alfredo. I'll do as you say. I'll go.
(He turns away.)

Violetta. So it's come to that already?
(She takes a flower from her corsage.)
Take this flower.

Alfredo. Why?

Violetta. So that you can bring it back to me.

Alfredo. (turning back) When?

Violetta. When it's withered.

Alfredo. You mean . . . tomorrow?

Violetta. Very well, tomorrow.

Alfredo. (rapturously taking the flower) I'm happy . . .
Oh, so happy!

LIBRETTO FROM *LA TRAVIATA*, GIUSEPPE VERDI, 1813-1901

THE Camellia is named after George Joseph Camellus, a Jesuit from Moravia. They are native to India, China and Japan where he travelled, and the flowers are often depicted in Oriental Art. They were featured in Alexander Dumas' book *The Lady of the Camellias* where the heroine conveyed her feelings to her suitors by wearing red or white camellias. The meaning of the White Camellia is Unpretending Excellence.

COLUMBINE
Folly

Ophelia. There's rosemary, that's for remembrance; pray you, love, remember. And there is pansies, that's for thoughts.

Laertes. A document in madness—thoughts and remembrance fitted.

Ophelia. There's fennel for you, and columbines. There's rue for you; and here's some for me. We may call it herb of grace a Sundays. O, you must wear your rue with a difference. There's a daisy. I would give you some violets, but they wither'd all when my father died. They say 'a made a good end.

HAMLET, WILLIAM SHAKESPEARE, 1564-1616

Poor mad Ophelia rightly carried columbines in her arms, for Shakespeare was well versed in the Language of Flowers and columbines were perfect for the bouquet of a deserted lover. The red flower signifies Anxiety and the purple, Resolution.

In the country it is known as Granny's Bonnet and the

genus name, *Aquilegia*, is from the Latin word for eagle, the base of the flower resembling an eagle's claws. It reminded others of a flight of doves for it was named Columbine from the Latin "columba" meaning dove. It is also due to this association that the flower has become a symbol of the Holy Spirit and appears often in religious paintings by the great masters.

DAFFODIL
Regard and Chivalry

I wandered lonely as a cloud
That floats on high o'er vales and hills,
When all at once I saw a crowd,
A host of golden daffodils;
Beside the lake, beneath the trees,
Fluttering and dancing in the breeze.

Continuous as the stars that shine
And twinkle on the milky way,
They stretched in never-ending line
Along the margin of a bay:
Ten thousand saw I at a glance,
Tossing their heads in sprightly dance.

WILLIAM WORDSWORTH, 1770–1850

Wordsworth's famous lines have immortalised the
Daffodil and there is hardly a poet in our language
who has not written of it.

It is said that the name Daffodil probably comes from
Affodyle, an old English word meaning early-comer. In
Shakespeare's day it had many nicknames such as

daff-a-down-dilly and daffodilly and it is also known as
the Lent lily. Some regard it as unlucky to have them in
the house for they hang their heads and bring tears and
unhappiness. This may have come from the Story of
Proserpina, told by Perdita in *The Winter's Tale*, who was
captured whilst picking lilies and carried off by Pluto, the
Greek god. In her fear Proserpina dropped the lilies and
they turned into daffodils as they touched the ground.

DAISY

Innocence

I'd choose to be a daisy,
 If I might be a flower;
Closing my petals softly
 At twilight's quiet hour;
And waking in the morning,
 When falls the early dew,
To welcome Heaven's bright sunshine,
 And Heaven's bright tear-drops too.

I'D CHOOSE TO BE A DAISY. ANONYMOUS

THE Daisy is the children's flower. They love to
gather it for posies and for making daisy chains. It is
also known as Baby's-pet or Bairn-wort meaning child-
flower. If a little girl picks a bunch of daisies with her
eyes shut, the number of flowers in the posy will be the
number of years before she marries. Young girls have
always told their fortunes by pulling the petals off to the
refrain "He loves me, he loves me not".

It is quite true to its name, for in the morning it opens
with the light of day and when the sun goes down it folds
up its white petals again as if it were going to sleep. Daisy
means the day's eye, or the eye of the day.

FORGET-ME-NOT

True Love

From off her glowing cheek, she sate and stretched
The silk upon the frame, and worked her name
Between the Moss-rose and the Forget-me-not—
Her own dear name, with her own auburn hair!
That forced to wander till sweet spring return,
I yet might ne'er forget her smile, her look,
Her voice, (that even in her mirthful mood
Has made me wish to steal away and weep.)
Nor yet the entrancement of that maiden kiss
With which she promised, that when spring returned,
She would resign one half of that dear name
And own thenceforth no other name but mine!

THE KEEP SAKE. SAMUEL TAYLOR COLERIDGE. 1772-1834

THE flower is associated with loving remembrance and true love. Once upon a time a knight in armour was walking along the bank of a river with his lady. She saw some flowers growing at the edge of the water and asked him to pick them for her. As the knight stretched out his hand for them, he slipped and fell into the river. Wearing heavy armour, he was unable to swim and was carried away down stream but not before he had thrown the flowers onto the bank for her. Forget-me-not! he cried as he drifted away. The maiden never forgot him and called the flower Forget-me-not in his memory.

The Forget-me-not gets its botanical name *Myosotis scorpioides* from the idea that the leaves resemble the ears of mice; all the plants of this family are known as Scorpion Grass because their clusters of flowers curl upwards like the tail of a scorpion.

GERANIUM

Beautiful Evelyn Hope is dead!
Sit and watch by her side an hour.
That is her book-shelf, this her bed;
She plucked that piece of geranium-flower,
Beginning to die too, in the glass;
Little has yet been changed, I think:
The shutters are shut, no light may pass
Save two long rays thro' the hinge's chink.

But the time will come,—at last it will,
When, Evelyn Hope, what meant (I shall say)
In the lower earth, in the years long still,
That body and soul so pure and gay?
Why your hair was amber, I shall divine,
And your mouth of your own geranium's red—
And what you would do with me, in fine,
In the new life come in the old one's stead.

ROBERT BROWNING. 1812-1889

Geraniums are to be found in most parts of the world and almost everywhere are confused with Pelargoniums. Their botanical name comes from the Greek word "geranos", meaning a crane, for the fruit of the plant resembles a crane's beak, hence the nickname Cranesbill. Geraniums are said to have been given their colour by Mohammed who left his clothes to dry on a bed of mallow. The flowers blushed dark red with pride and never lost their colour, and have been known as geraniums ever since. I always associate them with the Mediterranean where they tumble out of terracotta pots and down painted stone walls, the very colour of them creating a festive mood.

HONEYSUCKLE
Sweetness of Disposition

Ye have been fresh and green,
Ye have been fill'd with flowers:
And ye the Walks have been
Where Maids have spent their houres.

Y'ave heard them sweetly sing,
And seen them in a Round:
Each Virgin, like a Spring,
With Hony-succles crown'd.

But now, we see, none here,
Whose silv'rie feet did tread,
And with dishevell'd Haire,
Adorn'd this smoother Mead.

Like Unthrifts, having spent,
Your stock, and needy grown,
Y'are left here to lament
Your poore estates, alone.

ROBERT HERRICK, 1591-1674

*Y*ou have only to suck the honey out of the centre of the flower to see where the Honeysuckle got its name and meaning. Very sweetly scented, it is beloved by poets for its virtues and mentioned frequently by Shakespeare who often called it by the country name of Woodbine. Its woody stems twine clockwise around anything in its path, and true to its herbal name, *Caprifolium*, the flower climbs as nimbly as a goat.

Often growing in the wild, it transforms its surroundings into a place of floral enchantment by its evocative scent.

HYACINTH

Sorrow

Yet art thou not inglorious in thy fate;
For so Apollo, with unweeting hand
Whilome did slay his dearly-loved mate
Young Hyacinth born on Eurotas' strand,
Young Hyacinth the pride of Spartan land;
But then transform'd him to a purple flower
Alack that so to change thee winter had no power.

JOHN MILTON, 1608-1674

Ｉｎ Greek mythology there was a handsome boy from Sparta called Hyacinthus. He was a great friend of Apollo, the sun god, who would descend to the earth from his golden chariot in the sky to play with him. One day the two friends were competing to see who could throw the discus the furthest. They were watched by Zephyrus, the god of the wind. He was jealous of Apollo, for he was fond of Hyacinthus and he plotted his revenge. Next time Apollo threw the heavy circular disc, Zephyrus blew the West Wind causing the disc to go off course and strike Hyacinthus a fatal blow on the head. Apollo was filled with grief at the death of his friend and created hyacinths out of the blood which had been shed. Thus Apollo ensured that the memory of his friend would live on.

IRIS
Message

Thou art the Iris, fair among the fairest,
Who, armed with golden rod
And winged with the celestial azure, bearest
The message of some God.

Thou art the Muse, who far from crowded cities
Hauntest the sylvan streams,
Playing on pipes of reed the artless ditties ·
That come to us as dreams.

O flower-de-luce, bloom on, and let the river
Linger to kiss thy feet!
O flower of song, bloom on, and make for ever
The world more fair and sweet.
HENRY WADSWORTH LONGFELLOW, 1807–1882

*I*RIS was the messenger of the ancient Greek gods and she appeared to the mortals on earth in the form of a rainbow. The glorious arc was said to be the flight of Iris winging a message across the sky. She was as fleet of foot as the bloom of the flower is short, and there are as many different shades of the Iris as there are colours of the rainbow.

The Iris had many admirers, including the kings of France who used it as their royal emblem, and called it the Fleur-de-Lis. Shakespeare often referred to the flower in his plays by the anglicised name Flower-de-Luce.

JASMINE

Yellow Jasmine – Grace and Elegance
White Jasmine – Amiability
Spanish Jasmine – Sensuality

My pensive Sara! thy soft cheek reclined
Thus on mine arm, most soothing sweet it is
To sit beside our cot, our cot o'ergrown
With white-flowered Jasmin, and the broad-leaved Myrtle,
(Meet emblems they of Innocence and Love!)
THE ÆOLIAN HARP. SAMUEL TAYLOR COLERIDGE. 1772-1834

THE name comes from the Arabic, "jas" meaning despair and "min" meaning a lie. It is as famous for its scent as its flower, having an exotic, heady perfume which is especially intoxicating at night. The Hindus gave it the beautiful name Moonlight of the Grove.

LILAC
First Emotions of Love

O were my Love yon lilac fair,
Wi' purple blossoms to the spring,
And I a bird to shelter there,
When wearied on my little wing;
How I wad mourn when it was torn
By autumn wild and winter rude!
But I wad sing on wanton wing
When youthfu' May its bloom renew'd.

ROBERT BURNS, 1759–1796

THE Lilac is a member of the olive family but it used to be known as Blue-pipe in allusion to the hollow stems which were used for pipes. The name comes from the Greek word "syringa" meaning tube and it is probable that the plant originated in Greece or Southern Europe. But it has become a great favourite in England and has been widely planted here since the time of Henry VIII.

Country people call it May Flower and Lily-oak and many are superstitious about bringing it indoors, particularly the white variety whose meaning is Youthful Innocence. Like many white flowers it is also associated with death and indeed it refuses to bloom if another lilac is cut down in the garden.

It is curious that in the Language of Flowers the Lilac should symbolise such pure sentiments for in some villages a lilac branch is said to signify a broken engagement.

LILY
Purity

And the stately lilies stand
Fair in silvery light
Like saintly vestals, pale in prayer;
Their pure breath sanctifies the air,
As its fragrance fills the night.
ANONYMOUS

THE Lily has always been regarded as the symbol of purity and is one of the oldest flowers in the world. It may be found painted on the walls of ancient Greek palaces where it was the personal flower of Hera, the moon goddess.

The Lily is dedicated to the Virgin Mary in honour of her purity which is perhaps why many brides like to include it in their bouquets, and why it may be found at many religious festivals. Legend has it that the first lily sprang up from the tears dropped by Eve when she left the Garden of Eden.

LILY OF THE VALLEY
Return of Happiness

My heart aches, and a drowsy numbness pains
My sense, as though of hemlock I had drunk,
Or emptied some dull opiate to the drains
One minute past, and Lethe-wards had sunk :
 'Tis not through envy of thy happy lot,
 But being too happy in thine happiness,—
That thou, light-winged Dryad of the trees,
 In some melodious plot
Of beechen green, and shadows numberless,
Singest of summer in full-throated ease.

ODE TO A NIGHTINGALE, JOHN KEATS, 1795–1821

*I*т is not surprising that the Lily of the Valley symbolises the Return of Happiness for it is the sweetest flower imaginable. With its dainty white bells and unmistakable green scent it is said to lure the nightingale from his nest and lead him to his mate.

It is the symbol of May Day and was known as May Lily and Our Lady's Tears because it grew from the tears shed by the Virgin Mary at the Cross. The flowers were grown by monks for decorating the altar and were called Ladder to Heaven because the miniature flower-bells grow like steps up the stem.

MARIGOLD
Grief

Open afresh your round of starry folds,
    Ye ardent marigolds!
Dry up the moisture from your golden lids,
    For great Apollo bids
That in these days your praises should be sung
On many harps, which he has lately strung;
And when again your dewiness he kisses,
Tell him, I have you in my world of blisses:
So haply when I rove in some far vale,
His mighty voice may come upon the gale.

JOHN KEATS 1795–1821

The Marigold, *Calendula*, has always been associated with the sun's journey across the sky, from nine in the morning until three in the afternoon. The Victorians believed they could set the clock by the hour the Marigold opened and closed its colourful petals. *Calendula* is the name of the genus because it flowers all round the calendar year, and the name Marigold probably means Mary-gold after the Virgin Mary. In some parts they are also known as Mary-bud and Mary-gold. Lots of children have been reminded of a button when looking at the big, round flower, and so have called them Bachelor's Buttons, a name they share with several other members of the daisy family.

The Marigold signifies Grief, it is believed, because the flower daily mourns the departure of the sun when its petals are forced to close.

NARCISSUS
Egotism

What first inspired a bard of old to sing
Narcissus pining o'er the untainted spring?
In some delicious ramble, he had found
A little space, with boughs all woven round;
And in the midst of all, a clearer pool
Than e'er reflected in its pleasant cool,
The blue sky here, and there, serenely peeping
Through tendril wreaths fantastically creeping.
And on the bank a lonely flower he spied,
A meek and forlorn flower, with naught of pride,
Drooping its beauty o'er the watery clearness,
To woo its own sad image into nearness:
Deaf to light Zephyrus it would not move;
But still would seem to droop, to pine, to love.
So while the poet stood in this sweet spot,
Some fainter gleamings o'er his fancy shot;
Nor was it long ere he had told the tale
Of young Narcissus, and sad Echo's bale.

JOHN KEATS. 1795–1821

ORCHID
A belle

I met a lady in the meads
Full beautiful, a faery's child;
Her hair was long, her foot was light,
And her eyes were wild.

I set her on my pacing steed,
And nothing else saw all day long;
For sideways would she lean, and sing
A faery's song.

I made a garland for her head,
And bracelets too, and fragrant zone;
She look'd at me as she did love,
And made sweet moan.

She found me roots of relish sweet,
And honey wild, and manna dew;
And sure in language strange she said,
I love thee true.

LA BELLE DAME SANS MERCI. JOHN KEATS. 1795-1821

We think of orchids as exotic flowers, the product of hothouses and warm climes, but there are a lot of smaller orchids which grow wild in English fields and hedgerows. All orchids have spots, their very own beauty marks, and folklore tells us that there were orchids growing at the foot of the Cross when Jesus was crucified. His blood dropped on the flowers and they have carried the stain ever since.

As different species have varying blooms of curious shapes, so the Orchid has been named Adder's-tongue, Dead Men's Fingers, Ram's-horns and variously after Mother Goose and her goslings, Giddy-gander and Goosie-gander, on account of the way the flowers are grouped on the stem. Orchids are highly prized and quite unique, as their language implies.

PANSY
Thoughts

I send thee pansies while the year is young,
    Yellow as sunshine, purple as the night;
Flowers of remembrance, ever fondly sung
    By all the chiefest of the sons of light;
        And if in recollection lives regret
For wasted days, and dreams that were not true,
I tell thee that the pansy "freaked with jet"
Is still the heart's-ease that the poets knew.
Take all the sweetness of a gift unsought,
And for the pansies send me back a thought.

SARAH DOUDNEY

*P*ANSY is just an English way of saying the French word "pensée" which means thought, and people used to send these flowers for their nearest and dearest to remember them by. The small velvet plants we grow in our summer borders were first bred in Victorian times from the Wild Pansy which Shakespeare described as Love-in-idleness. This little flower with the smiling face was said to be a love potion, and was the cause of Titania falling in love with an ass in *A Midsummer Night's Dream*.

Wild Pansy has always been a favourite with children and country folk who have given it many affectionate names – Two-faces-under-the-sun, Face-and-hood and Tickle-my-fancy. It has also been called Herb Trinity, because there are often three colours in the one flower, reminding us of the Holy Trinity. Perhaps the best known of all the names, however, is Heartsease, for it was believed that by carrying the flower about with you, you would ensure the love of your sweetheart.

PRIMROSE
Early Youth

Perdita. Now, my fair'st friend,
I would I had some flow'rs o' th' spring that might
Become your time of day—and yours, and yours,
That wear upon your virgin branches yet
Your maidenheads growing. O Proserpina,
For the flowers now that, frighted, thou let'st fall
From Dis's waggon! . . .
. . . pale primroses,
That die unmarried ere they can behold
Bright Phœbus in his strength—a malady
Most incident to maids

THE WINTER'S TALE. WILLIAM SHAKESPEARE. 1564-1616

THERE are few flowers whose coming is so eagerly awaited in the year as the Primrose and it is because it is one of the early signs of spring that it received its name which means "first rose". It is not what we would call a rose today, but long ago the name was used more widely. In parts of western England the Primrose is still called the Butter-rose, because the colour of the flowers is so like that of the farmhouse butter which is made there.

Primroses became very fashionable in Victorian times and were Disraeli's favourite flower. Queen Victoria sent him many bunches from her gardens during her reign, and on his death she sent a large wreath of Primroses as a token of her affection and respect.

ROSE

Rose – Love
White Rose – Purity and Spiritual Love
Yellow Rose – Decrease of Love and Infidelity
Cabbage Rose – Ambassador of Love
Musk Rose – Capricious Beauty
Single Rose – Simplicity

If Jove would give the leafy bowers
A queen for all their world of flowers,
The rose would be the choice of Jove,
And blush the queen of every grove.
Sweetest child of weeping morning,
Gem, the breast of earth adorning,
Eye of flow'rets, glow of lawns,
Bud of beauty, nursed by dawns:
Soft the soul of love it breathes,
Cypria's brow with magic wreathes;
And to Zephyr's wild caresses,
Diffuses all its verdant tresses,
Till glowing with the wanton's play,
It blushes a diviner ray.

SAPPHO OF LESBOS. *c.* 600 BC.

SUNFLOWER
Haughtiness

No, the heart that has truly lov'd never forgets,
But as truly loves on to the close,
As the sun-flower turns on her god, when he sets,
The same look which she turn'd when he rose.

THOMAS MOORE, 1779-1852

THE Sunflower surely has a right to feel haughty for it is by far the tallest plant in the garden. Its size is not its only asset, however, for every part of the plant is used in some way: the seeds for eating and making oil and soap; the leaves and stalks for fodder and making cloth and even as a substitute for tobacco.

The genus name of *Helianthus* comes from two Greek words, "helios" meaning sun and "anthos" meaning flower. It was worshipped as the symbol of the sun by the Incas of Peru and later by the North American Indians. There is a classical legend that Clytie, a water nymph, was changed into a sunflower having died of a broken heart at the betrayal of Apollo, the sun god.

Other names include the Marigold of Peru and the Indian Sun, but my favourite is the Italian name "Girasole" because the flowers really do turn their heads to follow the sun's daily course from east to west.

TULIP

Red Tulip – Declaration of Love
Variegated Tulip – Beautiful Eyes
Yellow Tulip – Hopeless Love

But love, first learned in a lady's eyes,
Lives not alone immured in the brain,
But, with the motion of all elements,
Courses as swift as thought in every power,
And gives to every power a double power,
Above their functions and their offices.
It adds a precious seeing to the eye ;
A lover's eyes will gaze an eagle blind ;
A lover's ears will hear the lowest sound,
When the suspicious head of theft is stopp'd :
Love's feeling is more soft and sensible
Than are the tender horns of cockled snails :
Love's tongue proves dainty Bacchus gross in taste.
For valour, is not love a Hercules,
Still climbing trees in the Hesperides ?
Subtle as Sphinx ; as sweet and musical
As bright Apollo's lute, strung with his hair ;
And when Love speaks, the voice of all the gods
Makes heaven drowsy with the harmony.
Never durst poet touch a pen to write
Until his ink were temper'd with Love's sighs.

LOVE'S LABOUR'S LOST. WILLIAM SHAKESPEARE. 1564-1616

*N*o flower has gone in and out of vogue quite so much as the Tulip. Condemned for many years in England to town parks and railway station gardens, they are now once again appreciated for their glorious colours and party-frock petals. Cultivated and prized like jewels by the Turks and highly regarded also by the Persians, their name comes from the Persian word "tulipant" meaning turban which was used to describe the shape of the flower. They were introduced into European gardens in the Sixteenth Century and were generally welcomed, but it

was Holland that took the flower to its heart, and its
pocket, and the cultivation and buying and selling of
bulbs reached such a frenzy that the economy of the
country was put in jeopardy. Several decades later the
hysteria hit England where the government was forced to
pass a law limiting the price of a single bulb to four
hundred old English pounds.

Tulips are grown solely for pleasure, having no value
for the herbalist. They did finally make themselves useful,
however, when the hungry peoples of occupied Europe
were reduced to eating them during the war.

VIOLET
Modesty

For Hamlet, and the trifling of his favour
Hold it a fashion, and a toy in blood ;
A violet in the youth of primary nature
Forward, not permanent, sweet, not lasting,
The perfume and suppliance of a minute ;
No more.

HAMLET, WILLIAM SHAKESPEARE, 1564–1616

THIS humble flower has been celebrated in poetry and romance from ancient times and is much loved for its delicate powdery scent. It was widely referred to by Shakespeare, who called it "forward", for it blooms early and heralds the approach of summer. The plant is often described as modest for hiding its dark beauty away in the long grass and for flowering so fleetingly.

There are many stories regarding the Violet's name, but it almost certainly originated in Greece where it was considered the flower of Zeus, the king of the gods. Legend has it that Zeus was in love with a beautiful maiden called Io and in order to protect her from Hera, his jealous wife, he changed her into a beautiful calf. Then in order to feed her with delicacies, he commanded the earth to bring forth a beautiful flower in her honour, which he named Ion, the Greek word for Viola.

WATER LILY
Purity of Heart

Now folds the lily all her sweetness up,
And slips into the bosom of the lake :
So fold thyself, my dearest, thou, and slip
Into my bosom and be lost in me.
ALFRED, LORD TENNYSON, 1809–1892

WATER Lilies take their name from the Greek water nymph, Nymphe, the goddess of springs, as they were found growing where the nymphs were said to play. Their language reflects the delicacy of the pure white flower which does not open until midday then retires in early evening.

PICTURE ACKNOWLEDGEMENTS

In order of appearance

Jacket : *Dame Alice Ellen Terry* by George Fredrick Watts, National Portrait Gallery, London. Back jacket : *The Bunch of Lilacs*, James Jacques Tissot, Christies London, Bridgeman Art Library.

Portrait of a Girl in a Blue Cloak, Emma Sandys/Private Collection, Bridgeman Art. *Birthday Greetings*, Raimondo De Madrazo, Fine Art Photographic Library. *Amaryllis*, Mrs Loudon's Bulbous Plants, Royal Horticultural Society. *The Pet Bunny*, James Thomas Watts, Fine Art Photographic Library. *The Bluebell Wood*, Charles Haigh-Wood, Fine Art Photographic Library. *The Swallow Track*, E Richardson, Fine Art Photographic Library. *Dame Alice Ellen Terry* by George Fredrick Watts, National Portrait Gallery, London. *Dreams*, Sir Frederick William Burton, Fine Art Photographic Library. *The Swallow Track*, Beatrice Parsons, Some English Gardens by Gertrude Jekyll and G S Elgood. *A Lazy Afternoon*, David Fulton, Fine Art Photographic Library. *Sweethearts*, Frederick Morgan A & F Pears Ltd, London, Bridgeman Art Library. *Love's Shadow*, Anthony Frederick August Sandys, Christies London, Bridgeman Art Library. *Arranging Flowers*, Edgar Bundy, Eaton Gallery London, Bridgeman Art Library. *Honeysuckle*, Curtis's Botanical Magazine, Royal Horticultural Society. *Sir John and Lady Strickland*, Arthur Devis, Ferens Art Gallery Hull, Bridgeman Art Library. *Hyacinth*, Curtis's Botanical Magazine, Royal Horticultural Society. *Absence makes the heart grow fonder*, Marcus Stone, Fine Art Photographic Library. *In the Garden*, Frederick Jackson, Christopher Wood Gallery. *Spring*, Lucas van Valkenborch, Private Collection, Bridgeman Art Library. *Lilac*, Davidson Knowles, Christopher Wood Gallery London, Bridgeman Art Library. *The Bunch of Lilacs*, James Jacques Tissot, Christies London, Bridgeman Art Library. *Carnation, Lily, Lily, Rose*, John Singer Sargent, Tate Gallery. *Convent Thoughts*, Charles Allston Collins, Ashmolean Museum, E.T. Archive. *Lilies of the Valley*, Fine Art Photographic Library. *The March Marigold*, Edward Burne Jones, Piccadilly Gallery London, Bridgeman Art. *The Mirror*, Florent Willems, Galerie George London, Bridgeman Art Library. *Portrait of a Girl*, Sir Frank Dicksee, Fine Art Photographic Library.

PENHALIGON'S VIOLETTA

*T*HE Language of Flowers has been scented for your pleasure with Violetta. The Victorians were very fond of violets and flower sellers with baskets full of the small purple bunches were a common sight on the streets of London.

Ever since the time of the Ancient Greeks the Violet has been recognized as something rare and desirable. That they are still in such demand today gives us an indication of the true worth of this modest flower with its powerful scent.

Sheila Pickles

PENHALIGON'S LANGUAGE OF FLOWERS

This revised edition published in Great Britain in 1994 by
PAVILION BOOKS LIMITED
26 Upper Ground, London SE1 9PD

Original edition published in Great Britain in 1990

4 6 8 10 9 7 5 3

Designed by Bernard Higton

Picture research by Lynda Marshall

A CIP record for this book is available from the British Library

ISBN 1 85793 300 1

Manufactured in China by Imago

For more information on Penhaligon's
perfumes, please write to :
PENHALIGON'S
41 Wellington Street
London WC2